Research Wise

Classroom Strategies that Build Information Skills

Naomi Roche

USER FRIENDLY RESOURCES
EDUCATIONAL PUBLISHERS
www.userfr.com

Published by User Friendly Resources

Book No. 548

TITLE

Book Name: Research Wise
– *Classroom Strategies that Build Information Skills*

Book Number: 548

ISBN Number: 1-86968-399-4

Published: 2007

AUTHOR

Naomi Roche

ACKNOWLEDGEMENTS

Designer: Glen Honeybone

Illustrator: Glen Honeybone

Editor: Scanlan Communications Ltd.

PUBLISHERS

User Friendly Resources Ltd.

UK Office
Freepost RRCB-ALHY-YAAA
User Friendly Resources
Parkside Farm
Shortgate Lane
Lewes
BN8 6DG
Ph: 0845-450-7502
Fax: 0845-450-7501

New Zealand Office
P.O. Box 1820
Christchurch
Phone: 0508-500-393
Fax: 0508-500-399

Australian Office
P.O. Box 914
Mascot, NSW 2020
Phone: 1800-553-890
Fax: 1800-553-891

WEBSITE

www.userfr.com

E-MAIL

info@userfr.com

User Friendly Resources specialises in publishing educational resources for teachers and students across a wide range of curriculum areas, at early childhood, primary and secondary levels. If you wish to know more about our resources, or if you think your resource ideas have publishing potential, please contact us at one of the above addresses.

Contents

About this Resource

Research Wise supports teachers and learners in using the practical skills needed to do *research and inquiry* learning. It consists of:

- Teacher information sheets (8)
- Student activities (30)
- Reinforcement activities (10+)
- Templates (13)

Though this resource could be used as a complete unit of work it is intended for teachers to use flexibly to match the learning needs of their students. For example, if students are asking lots of questions without using keywords, the teacher may go through 'Questions: Keywords' with students and then return to the topic of inquiry.

Similarly at the completion of a unit of inquiry a teacher may find that a student's learning was incomplete because they lacked an appropriate skill in one area. There should be an activity sheet here to support the teaching of that skill.

Undertaking inquiries or doing research involves; Asking Questions, Seeking Definitions, Searching for Information, Building Knowledge, Presentation and Evaluation. These components of research are interwoven and may take place several times within a particular study. Research skills are recursive rather than linear.

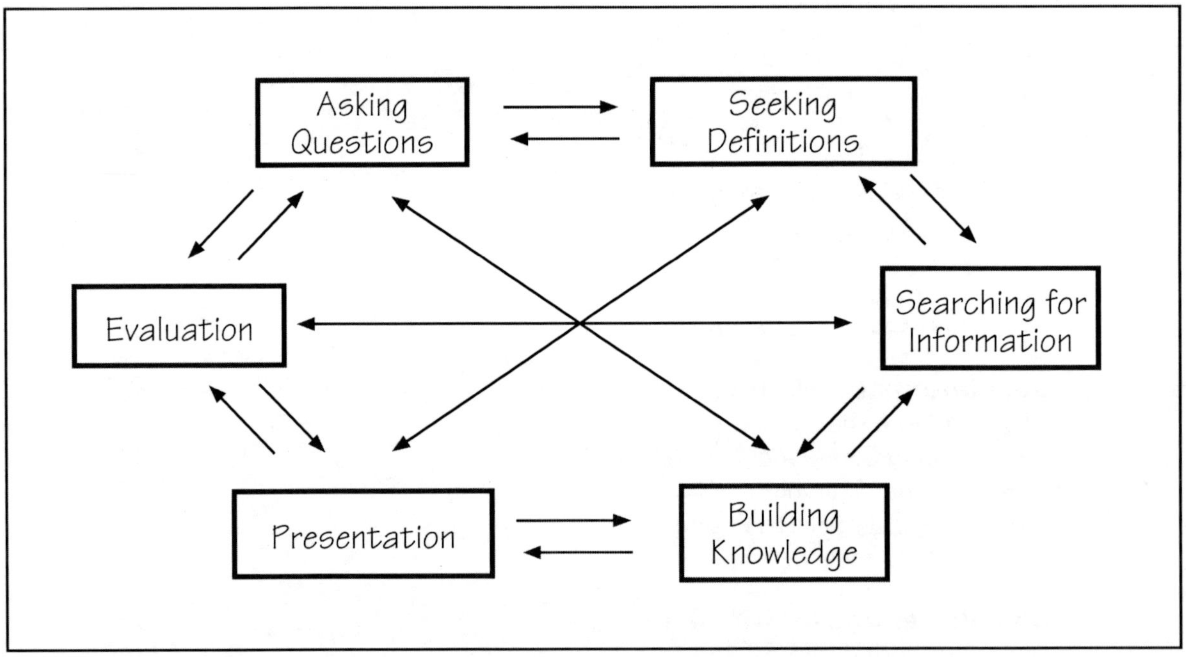

To assist teachers to identify what skills need support, both teacher and student tracking sheets are included at the end of this resource.

About Questions

Students have to learn how to ask questions that are meaningful and that will supply the information they want. For example, many students get 'stuck' using the same format for questions and some students will have issues identifying what information they actually need. They will not improve this skill without some targeted teaching.

One way to get students using different question formats is to have 'Question Starters' around the room, i.e.

"How do…?" **"When does…?"** **"How come…?"** **"What if…?"** **"Why?"**

Students can make the question starters themselves. It is also helpful to talk about types of questions. For example, 'How' questions tell you *how something happens*; 'when' questions tell you *what happens if* and/or *time frames* for something. A quick way to check is that most simple (as opposed to complex) questions begin with a question, followed by two nouns: **How** does the **sulphur** form in a **volcano**?' or a question followed by a noun and an adjective: **Why** is the **sea blue**?

It is very hard to formulate a question if you are not sure what you already know. Identifying the information that you need is part of the process of asking a question. There are activities in the **About Knowledge** section (p. 11) that may assist with this.

In whole-class inquiry and research topics the main question is often chosen by the teacher. The subsidiary questions that arise from this question are what we want students to formulate for themselves and then answer. Keeping track of these subsidiary questions for planning requirements can be tricky. It is useful to have them displayed around the room for planning purposes. A format to help keep track of questions is at the back of this resource.

Asking questions in a different way (rephrasing) can sometimes help student to better understand what information they need to answer it. Rephrasing questions can also elicit more information, as can making 'closed' questions into 'open' questions. For example, a closed question like "Can a lake be a sea?" could be rephrased as "What does a sea have that a lake does not?" Similarly, with more complex questions, students need to know what the keywords in a question are and how they relate. For example:

What are some of the differences between the sea and a lake?

How is the sea different from a lake?

These questions are asking for the same information, but they are using different structures to do so.

Activity 1: Keyword Questions A

Deciding what questions to ask can be tricky! Sometimes it helps to think about what you already know. Read through *What I Know About the Sea*. Circle all the **nouns** in red (naming words), **verbs** in blue (doing words) and **adjectives** in green (describing words with 'y' or 'ly' on the end). These are your *keywords*.

What I Know About The Sea

- The sea is salty.
- Lots of animals live in it.
- The sea has tides. They go up and down.
- It also has waves.
- There are lots of rocks and sand around the edge of the sea.

Now come up with as many ways to start a question as you can. For example, How does…? When did…? Why is…? Use the nouns, verbs and adjectives circled in *What I Know About the Sea* on the end of the question starters, like this…

What I Want To Know About The Sea

- **Why** is the sea salty?
- **How** does the sea get salty?
- **What** animals live in the sea?
- **When** do tides go up and down?
- **How** do the rocks and sand get around the edge of the sea?

Can you see a noun that has not been used in a question? Use that noun to create your own question about the sea.

My question is...

Compare your question with a friend. Did you come up with the same question? How are the questions similar or different?

Activity 2: Keyword Questions B

Write down everything you know about your topic.

What I already know about ____________________

To identify keywords, use different coloured pens to highlight all the nouns and verbs and adjectives in your sentences.

Think about the keywords, do you know *everything* about them? What more do you want to know about them? Write your questions below, using your keywords.

What I want to know about ____________________

1. ____________________

2. ____________________

3. ____________________

4. ____________________

Activity 3: Question Mapping

Where or When Questions

1. Where does the salt in the sea come from?
2. ______________________________

Why Questions

1. Why does the sea have salt in it?
2. ______________________________

Sea Salt

How Questions

1. How does the sea get salty?
2. ______________________________

Is and Does Questions

1. Does the salt in the sea have a special name?
2. ______________________________

It sometimes helps to 'map' questions to get more out of your topic. Above is an example of how you could map your questions. Add another question to each box. Try your own topic in the boxes below.

Where or When Questions

____

____

____

Why Questions

____

____

____

____

How Questions

____

____

____

____

Is and Does Questions

____

____

____

Activity 4: Questions: Open and Closed

Sometimes when we ask questions we get long and detailed answers, sometimes we get one word answers.

Closed questions are questions that only require a very short answer, usually yes or no. Closed questions are used in tests where there is a right and a wrong answer, but closed questions do not help you to find out a lot of information about a topic.

When you are trying to find out as much as possible about a topic it is better to use *open questions*. Open questions encourage people to list, describe, and sometimes give an opinion.

One way to tell closed and open questions apart is to think about how they may be answered. If the question can be answered in one word it is probably a closed question.

Can you tell which of the following questions are open? Put a tick beside the open questions (but don't try to answer them!)

☐ ***1.*** What makes the sea blue/green colour?
☐ ***2.*** Do you like the sea?
☐ ***3.*** Is there a name for how salty the sea is?
☐ ***4.*** If there is a name for how salty the sea is, what is it and how is it measured?
☐ ***5.*** Do fish live in the sea?
☐ ***6.*** What fish live in the sea?

Have a look at the closed questions on the left below and the same question asked as an open question on the right. Talk about why they are different.

Closed Question		*Open Question*
Are you OK?	→	How are you feeling?
Is all grass green?	→	Why is grass green?

Now try rewriting these closed questions as open questions:

Closed Question		*Open Question*
Do whales eat krill?	→	
Do all birds fly south for winter?	→	

Now try changing a closed question of your own into an open question.

	→	

Activity 5: Rephrasing Questions

Rephrasing a question means that you ask the same question in a different way. Why would you do this? We rephrase questions for a lot of reasons such as: to get better information, to get more specific information, to check we understand a question and because using the same form of question can get plain boring!

Have a look at this question.

Question		Rephrased Question
Why are you crying?	→	You're crying. Is there something wrong?

Will you get the same information from asking these two questions? ________________

What is different about the rephrased question? ________________

____

Read through the following transcript of an interview. Underline all the questions, then draw a line linking all the questions that are rephrased.

Jane's Interview with Mrs Gardener 98 years old : Childhood Toys and Games

What toys did you like to play with when you were little?

I liked to play hopscotch and dress ups with my doll.

Were there toys that you liked and played most with when you were young?

Yes, my doll and hopscotch strings.

Were girls allowed to play rugby?

Do you mean, did we play rugby or was it acceptable for us to play rugby?

Was it acceptable to play rugby?

No, not really. Rugby was considered very much a boy's game.

Did *you* ever play rugby?

Yes, but I got in to awful trouble with my mother. She was so cross as I ripped my new stockings.

Make a comment about the rephrased questions. Do rephrased questions help you to get the best infomration?

Write a question of your own and rephrase it.

About Knowledge

Students need to identify and evaluate what they know and don't know about a topic in order to learn. Being able to do this is part of the process of gaining new knowledge.

However asking students to write down everything they already know about a topic is likely to cause a lot of moaning and groaning... not to mention some valuable time wasted! In this part of the inquiry process, constructing mind maps (here, called knowledge maps) and undertaking individual brainstorms can be very valuable if done correctly. As such, some of this section focuses on clear and concise knowledge mapping and how to use these maps to find out what students don't know!

Knowledge maps can also be valuable assessment tools. Comparing knowledge maps done prior to topic immersion, after topic immersion and then post individual research makes a very visual statement of the students' deepening knowledge, and what aspects of the topic they have understood, learnt and remembered the most.

Have students do their initial map in blue pen and a subsequent map at the completion of their studies either on separate paper or in a different colour pen. Compare the two maps.

A student's ability to use written language may impede their willingness to map their knowledge. This can be overcome by having them talk about their topic for a set time, recording on video and then having them do this again at the end of the topic of study. Allow students to listen to both talks and evaluate their progress from this. This is also a great resource to have for students to demonstrate their learning to parents and caregivers at parent interviews!

It is very important to restrict time frames. Two minutes is long enough for each talk, some students will need prompts i.e. the person recording to verbally or visually remind them about types/ categories , the function or purpose. (Parent helpers and teacher aides are great for helping with the recordings). This can stop this process being too time consuming or anxiety causing. For more help with this see page 37.

Activity 6: Knowledge Maps A

How do you know what you don't know!? Writing down everything you know about a topic would take a very long time… unless you use a knowledge map to show what you know.

Knowledge maps show what's in your mind. You don't even need to worry about writing very much!

Some people will be confident enough with mapping to use a simple bubble topic to get them started. Have a go at this one. Put the name of a topic you know something about in the middle of this bubble. Then write seven facts that you know about your topic at the end of each of the lines that radiate from the bubble.

Freeform Map

It can be helpful to have subtopics for knowledge maps. This allows you to group your information. Here is an example:

Subtopic Map

Try using ONE of the two knowledge map formats above to note down what you know about the topic of Farm Animals. Can you think of better subtopics?

Activity 7: Knowledge Maps B

Look at the statements Stacey has made about **dogs**. Arrange the statements below on the format underneath. Try to group the statements under subtopics.

1. What subtopics might Stacey use to group her knowledge about dogs?

What I Know About Dogs

Dogs:
- Can be pets or wild
- Have puppies
- Are big types like German shepherds or mastiffs
- Can be small types like poodles and terriers
- Have fur, teeth and claws
- Farms have dogs
- Some dogs are working dogs
- Are part of the canine family

2. Use these knowledge statements to make up some subtopics and create a map of Stacey's knowledge. You may need more arrows and keep in mind that you should group similar information together!

Activity 8: Prior Written Knowledge

Let's find out how much you know about cats!

1. For one minute sit and think about cats.
2. When one minute is up, start grouping what you know about cats in the box below. You will only have two minutes to write so don't worry about spelling, or how to make it look nice, just write! Use subtopics to help you group your knowledge.

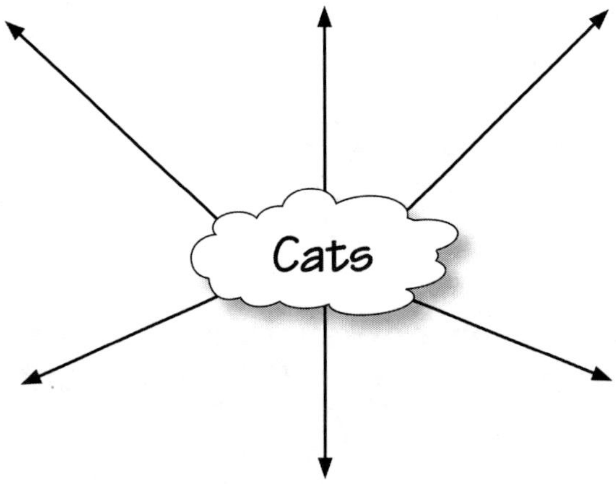

3. When you have written for two minutes stop, put down your pencil or pen and read what you have written. Have you missed anything out? Is there more that you would like to write? Think about this for one minute.
4. Now is your chance! You have two more minutes to add anything you think you may have missed.
5. When that two minutes is up you may want to share your knowledge map with a friend. Can you identify what things about cats you both know most about? Can you identify what things about cats you don't know much about?

Write down two other things you would like to know about cats.

1. ______________________________
2. ______________________________

Activity 9: Prior Oral Knowledge

Talking about what you know also shows how much you know about a topic. It can help if someone interviews you on your topic. Their questions will help to prompt you.

1. You will need a partner for this, and a clock or watch with a minute hand. One of you must be the interviewer (to time your talk and read prompts to you) and the other person will be the interviewee (the person doing the thinking and talking).

2. This time I have written the prompts for you! Each choose your topic, this should be something you know a bit about. Decide who will interview first and who will answer the questions.

3. You must both sit comfortably. The interviewer needs the prompts, a pen or pencil to make notes of things they want to mention later, something to put their paper on, and to be able to see a clock.

4. The interviewer asks the first question. Do not ask the next question until one minute is up, even if you have to sit in silence because the interviewee (person talking) does not have anything to say. When one minute is up ask the next question. Try not to talk over the interviewee; this is not good manners, but tell them when one minute is up.

Prompts

- Why have you chosen ________________ for your topic? (Time for one minute).
- Tell me between five and ten things about your topic. (Time for one minute).
- Choose one of those things and give me some more detail about it. (Time for one minute).
- Is there anything else about your topic that you would like to tell me?

When each of you has finished being interviewed, ask your partner if they have thought of anything that you didn't talk about.

5. Which do you prefer, *writing down* what you know, or *talking about* what you know?

6. Are there any other ways you could show someone what you know? Discuss this with some people in your class.

About Search Planning

After students have moved through the knowledge map and/or interview stage to determine what they already know, and don't know, they need to move onto search planning.

Getting ready to research is vital. It's not uncommon for enthusiastic students to go down a number of dead ends when they are searching for information about something. The result of not planning can be two-fold: frustration when accessible information seems elusive, and swamped when there seems to be too much information because the chosen topic is so enormous. These days we are in the happy position of having information literally at our fingertips; however, learning to search in a discerning way is a real skill.

These key questions can be used to shape the planning for a search. If you are setting up a whole-class inquiry, this process assumes that a research topic has already been chosen, and a Main Question has already been asked, students in this situation will be posing subsidiary questions (see p. 5).

1. What do I want to find out about? (pose the topic as a question)

2. What keywords do I need to use in my search?

3. Can I group these keywords in any way?

4. What sources of information are best for this search?

5. What is the best way to put my information together to demonstrate my knowledge and learning?

One way to open up a planning discussion with students is to ask them what advice they could give to a student who was interested in finding out more about Whales. How might this student plan for managing such an enormous topic? What kind of key question might help to focus the research?

Activity 10: Defining Search Terms

When we first start thinking about the topic that we want to research, we might think that we can just look it up on the Internet or in a book.

However, some of the problems that can happen when we do this are:

- Our topic could be too big and there might be too much information.
- We find the same information everywhere we look.
- We only use one search term for our topic, so only find part of the information.
- We only get information from one source.
- We search for information for so long that we have no time left to present it.

One of the best things to do when you start thinking about a research topic is to look up the topic's keyword in a good dictionary! Dictionaries are not only for checking spelling or the meaning of words! Let's pick the main topic word 'Cat' and see what the dictionary has to say.

> **Cat** *n.* **1.** Also called **domestic cat**. A small **feline** mammal of many **breeds**. Sometimes kept as pets or to get rid of vermin. **2.** Also called **feral cat**. Not familiar with humans. Wild cat. **3.** Also called **Big cat** any of the larger feline family such as lion, tiger.

From this dictionary entry I can get these helpful words.

cat **felines** **domestic** **breeds**

I know the topic of cats is too large though, so this definition helps me to narrow the focus to one thing that looks interesting or that is specific to the topic.

1. Now you try looking up the topic words below in the dictionary and listing the keywords (that could become search terms) that you find from the dictionary.

Dog	Volcano	France
1. ________	1. ________	1. ________
2. ________	2. ________	2. ________
3. ________	3. ________	3. ________
4. ________	4. ________	4. ________

2. Compare the different keywords and search terms you find with a partner.

Activity 11: Key Definitions

Like a dictionary, the thesaurus, encyclopaedia and atlas often contain valuable general information, keywords and search terms that can assist us in researching topic words. I have decided to research how cats became domesticated.

1. Have a look at the encyclopaedia entry for cats:

> ## Cats
>
> Cats are mammals of the feline family. The feline family includes both small cats and what are grouped as big cats. So the cat that you may have at home, a common domesticated cat is related to the great lions, tigers, leopards, and other big cats.
>
> Archaeological remains suggest that cats were first domesticated (lived with humans) in Egypt around 3,000 years ago. Cats in Egypt were treated like deities (gods) and were housed in temples.
>
> The benefits of having cats living with us were much more obvious back then as cats kept the numbers of disease carrying vermin, like rats and mice, down.
>
> Modern cats, though sometimes still kept for their abilities to keep vermin away, are more commonly kept for their companionship.
>
> There are hundreds of different breeds of domesticated cats. Some of the more common are the tabby and the Persian. Through careful breeding of cats to encourage certain qualities, such as the length of the tail, many different breeds have been established, such as the Manx cat which has no tail!

At this stage in our research we could take notes from this encyclopaedia, as this information would be helpful in building our general knowledge about cats. However, if the question I am trying to answer is how cats became domestic pets, the encyclopaedia doesn't give us enough to base our whole research around it, does it?

Though this extract does provide a number of keywords and phrases that will help us to search in books about cats, Internet sites, and people or organisations that may know about cats. With a highlighter, go through the encyclopaedia entry above and highlight the information that relates to how cats became domestic pets.

2. Write down all the keywords and phrases that could be used as search terms from this section in the box below.

Search terms from the encyclopaedia extract

3. How has the encyclopaedia helped in finding an answer to my research question?

Activity 12: The Research Plan

Planning makes perfect!
Have a look at the plan below for my research topic: How did cats become domestic pets?

Name: ______________ Date: ____/____/____

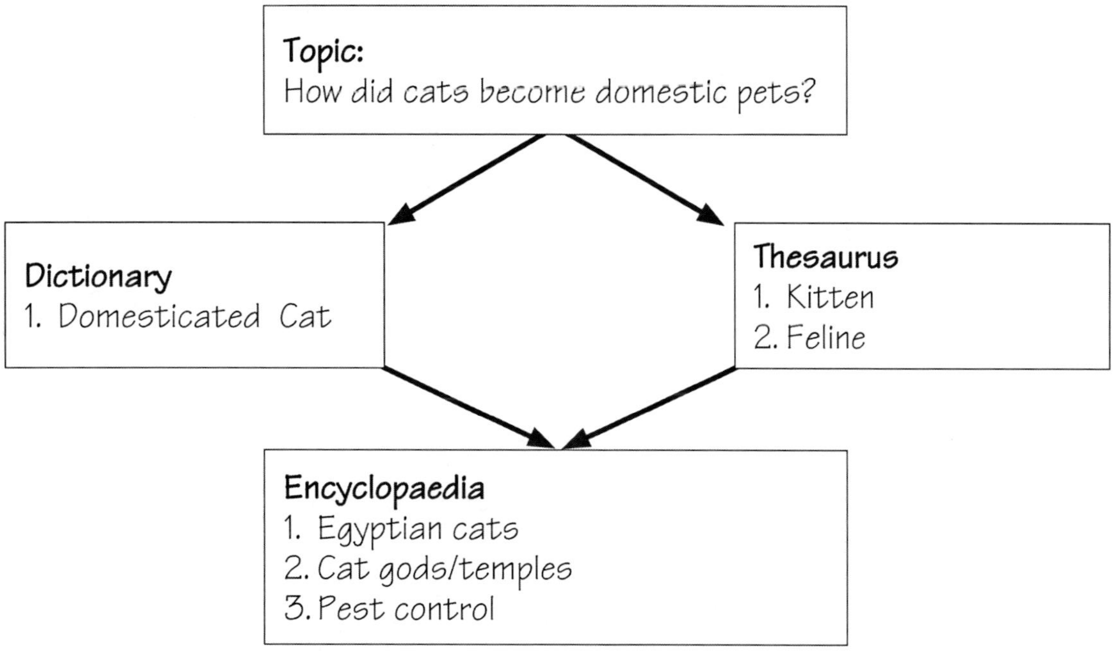

The next step is to start thinking about sources (places, books, Internet sites) that I already know of that may help me find answers.

With a partner start to think about places where I could find answers to my question, "How did cats become domestic pets?" Try to group information together by where it can be found. Be specific, I really need help!

You can find information in these places:

Activity 13: Time Frames

If you have ever tried to research something before, you will know how easy it is to get lost in mountains of information, sometimes not getting round to writing anything about your topic until the very last minute.

Finding information is only part of research, we need to make sure that we have time:

- to read the information
- understand the information
- present what we have found.

Have a look at how Jane thinks she will use the one week she has to complete an inquiry into the Olympic Games for homework.

Time Frames for: Olympic Games Inquiry **Name:** Jane Brain

Due Date: ___/___/___ **Date:** 30/03/08

________	Question Formulating
________	Definitions
________	Search Plan
________	Searching
________	• Library
________	• Internet
________	• Other
________	Evaluating
________	Reading / Note Taking
________	Presenting
________	Evaluating

1. On the left hand side list the number of minutes or hours she needs to spend on each task.

2. What should Jane spend the most time doing?________________

3. What should Jane spend the least time doing?________________

Generally we need to spend:

- **a third of our time** on questions, definitions, search plans and searching
- **a third of our time** on reading, note-taking and evaluating
- **and a third of our time** on presenting and evaluating.

Remember that evaluating can be something that happens several times during an inquiry or research topic!

About Search Recording

Getting into the habit of recording what searches they have made helps student to:

- trace their research path
- save time by not searching the same sources over again
- list references accurately
- avoid copying.

Reference librarians are very helpful if students are having trouble locating information on a particular topic, but most will expect them to know where they have already looked!

Copying (plagiarism) can be a real problem, not to mention the waste of time it creates for teachers marking work that is not the students' own. Encouraging students to reference their work can help them to become aware of using other people's ideas with acknowledgment to the author, as opposed to using other people's work and trying to use it as their own.

Some students may find it hard to work out what is fact and fiction let alone what is the accepted fact and the opinion. As students advance through school the distinctions between accepted fact and opinion will become much more necessary but the following activity introduces the concept of checking facts between at least a couple of sources, which can then be recorded.

Some students may be ready to begin discussing the idea, for example, recording the difference between 'source types', recording primary sources (someone's actual experience) and secondary sources (referring to someone's writing about another person's experience). The differences between the diaries of a soldier in World War Two (primary) as opposed to an article about World War Two is a good example of this.

A format sheet for the Search Recording is included in the Templates section at the back of this resource.

Activity 14: Bibliographies

When you are working on a project or doing some research, you have to get your information from somewhere, don't you? It doesn't just come out of your head! The world is filled with books, articles and websites that are dedicated to different topics. The people who have found out all this information are specialists in the areas they are writing about, so you will need to use their work to find out things you want to know. A bibliography is a list of titles that people have used to help them write their stuff. Even specialists need to consult other sources. You will see these at the end of just about any non-fiction writing. Readers can see where the writer's information has come from and will also know where to find other information on the subject. The word 'bibliography' comes from the Greek words *biblion* (book) and *graphia* (writing).

At school bibliographies are important to:

- show where we have looked for information
- acknowledge other writers' ideas that we are using
- help people who read our work to know where they can find some other useful information.

Have a look at the bibliography below.

Bibliography

Brown, S. (2003). *Caring for Dogs*. Penguin. London.
Manns, J. (2005). *A Dog's Life*. Harper Collins. Melbourne.
Smith, K. (2001). *The Dog Owner's Manual*. Leprechaun Publishing. Dublin.

Other Sources

www.doginfo.com

Answer these questions.

1. Why do you think the books listed alphabetically by the author's surname?

2. What are the numbers in brackets telling us?

3. What are the words that come after the title about?

4. Why do you think Other Sources are listed separately?

5. What do you think is special about the way the bibliography is set out?

6. Write these books as a bibliography.
- Auckland. Caring for Cats. (2003). G. White. SPCA Publishing.
- Capetown. John Smith. Cats Galore. (2001). Cat's Cradle Publishing.
- Penguin. A Cat's Life. M. Black. (1999). London.

Activity 15: Keeping Track

You need to keep track of where you have looked and where your information and notes have come from, otherwise it is very hard to write a bibliography or check facts later if you need to. It can also cause you to waste a lot of time searching the Internet or library catalogues only to find that you have already searched that book or site!

This student has got into good habits! Have a look at his search record. His research topic is Cat Breeds.

Search Words	Author/Date/Time/Publisher or Site	Comments
Cat	Black, M (2001) A Cat's Life. Penguin. London.	Chapter 7 (good)
	Brown, K (2003) Cats Galore. Mieow Books. Perth.	Sections 3, 4 and 8 (excellent and informative)
Feline	Tate, G (2005) The Feline Family. University Press. Auckland.	Pages 23-45 (hard to understand)
Google: Cat	www.catinfo.com	Too much stuff
	www.catland.com	Good pictures

Use these questions to discuss this search record.

1. Which book did this student find the most useful? ________________
2. Which book was probably more for adult readers? ________________
3. What is the name of the Internet site that they found helpful? ________________
4. Who is the author of *The Feline Family*? ________________
5. These search terms are a bit broad. Which terms would you have used? Can you help him out with a question? ________________

   ____

Your turn…

Imagine you are researching the topic of elephants. Think of a research question on this topic – it will probably begin with What, How, or When. Then search in your library catalogue (some catalogues of public libraries can be accessed on the Internet from your school). Use the space below to help keep track!

Research Question: ________________

Search	Author/Date/Time/Publisher or Site	Comments

Activity 16: Plagiarism

Plagiarism is copying someone else's writing and calling it your own. It's like stealing someone's thoughts. People that plagiarise other people's writing can get into very serious trouble. Have a look at the following two articles.

The Dark Ages

The Dark Ages or Middle Ages, as some call them, describe the period of time between the Classical period and the Renaissance.
A lot of things are attributed with causing the Dark Ages such as the fall of the Roman Empire. Though some also believe that the arrival of the black plague started the Dark ages.
The name 'The Dark Ages' describes the turning off of a mythical light of knowledge. Exactly as happened with the fall of the Roman Empire.
By Jim Init. 2007

Article 1

The Dark Ages

The Dark Ages span from the end of the collapse of the Roman Empire through to the beginning of the Renaissance. Both of which were centred in Rome.
The Dark Ages are sometimes called the Middle Ages, though the term Dark Ages better describes the conditions of the time.
With the fall of the Roman Empire, learning and art did not advance and the rudiments of modern medicine stopped progressing.
By Ridge Inal.2007

Article 2

Now have a look at Jane's paragraph about the Dark Ages for her research topic.

The Dark Ages

by Jane Kopy

The Dark Ages or Middle Ages as some call them describe the period of time between the classical period and the Renaissance. The Dark Ages end with the Renaissance as the Renaissance was the beginning of the rebirth of learning.

A lot of things are attributed with causing the Dark Ages such as the fall of the Roman Empire. The Roman Empire's main centre was in Italy and the Renaissance started in Italy. Many believe that Italy has been the centre of learning for the last two millennia. Regardless of this, the Dark Ages spread all across Europe. Art did not advance and the rudiments of modern medicine stopped progressing.

1. Underline the text that Jane has copied from the first article in blue.
2. Underline the text that Jane has copied from the second article in red.
3. How much of this article is Jane's work? ____________________
4. Does Jane tell us anywhere that she is using someone else's work? ____________________
5. What difference would it make if Jane wrote a bibliography (list of all the references she has used). ____________________
6. What difference would it make if Jane used quotation marks and said who she was quoting? ____________________
7. What do you think about copying other people's work and calling it your own? ____________________

Activity 17: Check Your Facts

Although non-fiction is supposed to be truthful, not all non-fiction that is written is fact. Some non-fiction represents someone's opinion, for example newspaper editorials. Even eye-witness accounts are just someone's opinion of what they saw.

In any information that you may read or hear there may be both facts and opinions. The difference between a fact and an opinion is that the fact can be proven and the other cannot. Since it can be impossible for us to prove things in class at school (like when the Renaissance actually happened) we have to base our facts on the facts of others. A quick way to check information is to 'cross check' with another source of information; like comparing two articles on the same topic. You can record in your bibliography that you have looked at both sources.

Read through the following two articles about the Renaissance.

The Renaissance

Renaissance means rebirth, and this is exactly what happened to learning in Europe in the years between 1350 AD and 1600 AD. After the Dark Ages, people again started being interested in learning and the arts. A lot of what they thought needed to be learned about was from classical times (Roman and Greek periods), before the Dark Ages. The Renaissance started in Italy and spread across Europe and around the world.

The Renaissance probably began in Florence, Italy.

The Rebirth of Learning

From the 1400s through to the beginning of the 1600s was a period called the Renaissance. Renaissance means rebirth. In this case it was the rebirth of learning and art from the classical times that had not been popular for several hundred years during the Dark Ages.

Starting in Italy and spreading across Europe the ideals of the Renaissance were adopted by many nations. As a result the new interest in learning and art produced some of the art that everyone considers to be masterpieces today.

1. Does Renaissance means rebirth? How do you know?

2. Find two things that the two articles agree on.

3. Is there anything that the articles differ on?

4. Is there anything in the either article that seems as though it could be an opinion of the writer, rather than a fact?

About Notetaking

Effective notetaking requires two skills. Firstly the ability to discern information by type i.e: fact or fiction, or to determine what is important or irrelevant. With some students it may also be appropriate to discuss the ideas of 'biased' and 'unbiased'. Secondly, the ability to retain and reproduce information meaning and context in an abbreviated way.

Categorising information is a very complex mental process. It is not something that can be taught through one activity. A student's ability to categorise is one indicator of their intellectual needs and I would urge you to investigate further if you find a student, over the age of eight is having difficulty categorising simple objects (i.e. apple, pear, orange are all fruit). Activity 18, following, on categorising information, may be quite difficult for some students. You may find it useful to adapt the phrases and try this as a daily activity for some time.

Though there are many formats in which to take notes such as symbols, images and words, students should take notes in a format that is suitable to the audience. Underlining and highlighting have the problem of still being part of a larger body of text. With this in mind, it is usually easier for students to use word-based formats so that they learn the importance of keeping the context and meaning of the text or words. Written notes are also more easily comprehended by teachers for marking. There is a short activity (Activity 19) about the selection of an audience-appropriate note style.

Emphasise to students that the subheadings and topic sentences from the books and articles they have used can shape their notes.

Similarly when students are using their notes to write reports they should be able to use main headings and paragraph topics as guides. It is also important at this stage to reiterate that their report should be in their words! If they are working from their notes their report will be different from the articles and books that they have used to get information.

Book Article → ***Student Notes*** → ***Student Report***

Cats and Dogs

Cats and dogs are **mammals**. This means that they have fur, are warm blooded, have live babies, and feed their babies milk. Cats are from a species (like a family) of animals called **felines**. The feline family includes lions and tigers. This doesn't mean that your family pet is a lion but that that millions of years ago they may have had an ancestor in common.

Cats **communicate** through their meows and their body position. Sometimes they even communicate through their claws!

Cats

Mammals
- -fur
- -warm blood
- - live babies
- - milk

Feline
- -lion, tiger

Cats

Cats are mammals. This means that they have warm blood, have fur, and have live kittens feed their kittens milk.

Cats are part of the animal family called felines. The feline family includes lions and tigers.

Activity 18: Categorising Information

A part of taking notes is grouping information together. Read the following statements and write them in the box that best suits their category.

Work with the police	Purr when they are happy	Guide the blind
Catch birds and mice	Herd cattle and sheep	Meow

Cats	Dogs

Have a look at the notes below and see if you can work out what has gone wrong.

Animals like dogs and cats
- Animals
  - Have claws
  - Meow
- Cats
  - are mammals

With a partner try to write these notes so that they make sense!

Activity 19: Types of Notes

There are many ways to take notes but some are more easily understood than others! We take notes to remind us about what we heard and read, and also so that other people know what we heard and read.

Have a look at my notes on 'Cows'. Then fill in the check list underneath to help you decide which type of notes *you* found easiest to understand.

A.

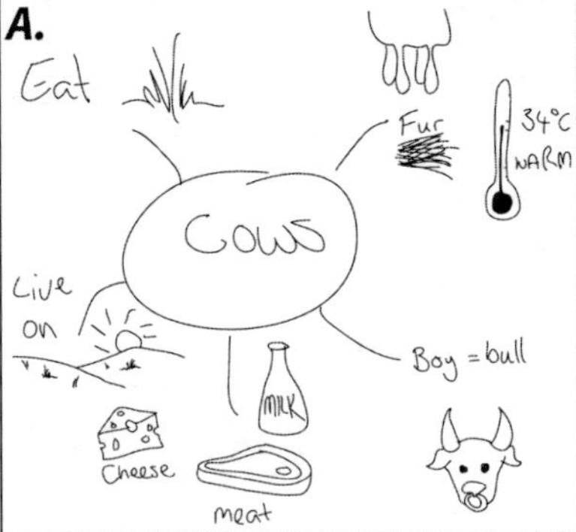

B.

COWS

Are
- mammals
- from bovine family

Farmed for
- meat (beef)
- dairy products (milk, cheese, butter etc.)

Eat
- grass and hay

C.

Cows are mammals so they have fur, feed live young, and have warm blood. Their family group is called bovine. This is the family of all types of cattle.
Cows are farmed for their meat which is called beef. They are also farmed for dairy products.
Dairy products are things like milk, cheese, and butter.
Cows eat mainly grass and hay.

Checklist

Colour the **best** in each category red, the **OK** in each category green, and the **worst** blue.

Category ↓ NOTES →	A	B	C
Has an easily identified topic			
Looks tidy			
Tells you the most information			
Is easiest to understand			
Takes up the least room on the page			

From the checklist:

1. Which type of notes are the easiest for you to understand?

____

2. Which type of notes are the hardest for you to understand?

____

3. Which type of notes do you think you might take for your reading or listening?

____

Activity 20: From Text to Notes

When you are taking notes from articles and books you can use the titles (chapter headings, section headings, side headings and so on) that are already in the text. This will help you to group together information so that it is easier to understand.

Another thing that makes note taking easier is to look at how the text or article has been paragraphed. This will also help you to group information together because paragraphs should only have one topic.

Look out for the keywords in an article or book. Make sure that you keep the context right though. Sometimes the keywords come up with auxiliary words like 'before' or 'after' – so you need to capture these too, or you might get the meaning wrong!

Have a look at the article below and the notes I have made from it. Can you see how I have done it? Draw a circle around the phrase or words that are in the article and draw an arrow pointing to where they are in my notes.

The Great Wall of China

The Great Wall of China is the longest fortification in the world. It was built to protect the Chinese Empire from nomadic tribes and the Mongol army.

The building of the Great Wall of China was begun in the 3rd century BC. It was still being built in the time of the Ming Dynasty in the 17th century. It took thousands of peasant labourers to build. Many of these labourers were buried inside the wall.

The wall is around 7,400 kilometres (4,600 miles) long, though most of this has crumbled away and there are only a few smaller sections that are still in good repair. These sections have been restored for tourists to visit. The section that is in the best repair is an 80 kilometre (50 miles) section in the Nankou Pass, just north of Beijing.

My Notes

The Great Wall of China

Fortification from

- nomad tribes
- Mongol army

Built

- between 3rd and 17th century
- by peasants
    - some buried there

Length

- around 7,400 km
- only small sections left
- some repaired for tourists
- Nankou Pass 80km

1. How have I done with my notetaking? Have I got anything confused?

2. What are some things that you notice are important in writing notes from text? (There are some clues in the instructions at the top of the page!)

3. What do you think will be the hardest thing about writing notes from things you have read?

Activity 21: From Notes to Text

Being able to use your notes to write full sentences and paragraphs is also a skill that takes practice.

Look at these notes that I wrote about the Island of Crete in Greece.

Crete
Geography
An Island
- largest of the Greek islands
- Capital – Heraklion
- Population 502,000 people
- speak Greek

History
- Minoan civilization 3500-1100 BC
  - lots of artifacts found
  - Minoans mysteriously disappeared
  - Worshipped bulls

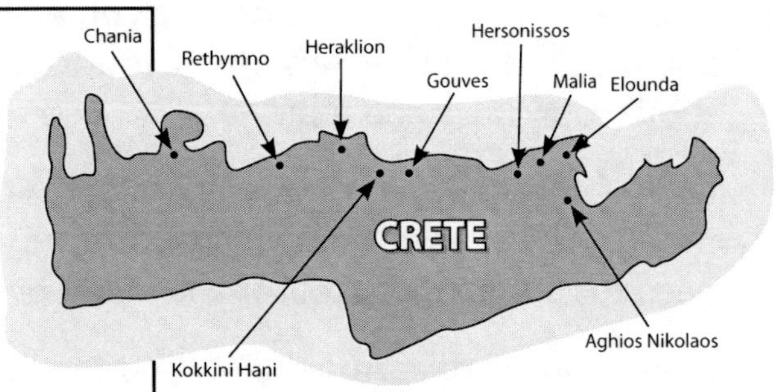

Try writing your own paragraphs on Crete using these notes.

Have a friend read your Crete paragraph and check that:

- You have used as much of the information as possible.
- You have written in full sentences.

Discuss with your friend

1. What the hardest thing about writing notes into a paragraph was for you.
2. What you need to remember when you are writing your own notes.
3. What you think is the most effective (easy to understand and use) way to gather notes so that you can use them for writing paragraphs from?

Activity 22: Notes from Interview

Like taking notes from written text, if you take notes from spoken words all the information must be sifted for its usefulness. The information you will use needs to be categorised and recorded in a way that will keep the meaning of the words.

Have a look at the transcript of an interview with Mrs Jones about toys that she played with in her childhood. The research topic is "What is the Difference Between Toys Then and Now?"

Because the student didn't have a tape recorder he had to listen carefully to what Mrs Jones said – and try to capture the main points in writing.

This is what the student heard:

Interview with Mrs Jones 30/3/07

What toys were popular for children in the 1950s?

Oh, the big craze at school was a game called elastics. I remember how we all used to play that. Though the boys didn't like to play elastics much. They preferred playing with marbles. Those boys could flick those marbles for yards.

2. Were there toys that you played with at home?

My father brought me home a beautiful doll one time. Not like the dolls today. It was hand sown with a cloth body and the head and face were made out of porcelain. It had a beautiful velvet dress. Of course I was only allowed to hold it after my bath at night, otherwise I may have got it dirty.

3. So the dolls weren't made of plastic?

This is what the student wrote down:

Interview 30/3/07
Mrs Jones
Place: her house

Toys 1950s
Popular at school
- Elastics (girls)
- Marbles (boys)

Popular at Home
Doll
- Porcelain, velvet, cloth (very strict use)

Read the interview and notes carefully. Highlight the words and phrases in the transcript and link them to where they are used in the notes. Do you think this student has done a good job or not?

Now you try!

Ask a friend to tell you about the best holiday they have had and three things that happened on the holiday. You try taking notes. When you have finished tell your friend about your holiday so that they can try writing notes.
Check each other's notes.
Did you get the main points they talked about?

About Information Sources

Identifying appropriate sources of information is a skill central to the research and inquiry process. Students need to understand the different types of information available to them but also to know their advantages and limitations.

The quality of students' research can be directly affected by the sources they have used and different students will have different skills. With this in mind this section is intended to give a basic summary of possibilities and processes.

Access to computers will be needed for some of the research, such as Internet searching. Teachers need to check their schools' Internet policy and permissions. If giving students open access to the Internet is not an option it may be possible to save listings from search engines such as Google to an in-school intranet. To fulfil the idea of the activity (selecting information) it would be important to include some less relevant sites on the intranet.

Similarly, a check of your school's policies on students phoning, faxing and emailing may be in order. If there are issues with students contacting people, it may be possible to 'prime' or organise a situation so that students still get the experience of using their phone, fax or email skills.

Some libraries now have their catalogues (book listings) on the Internet, so while the library activities will not necessarily need to be done in a library, it would be more effective.

Activity 23: Get into the Library

Libraries are designed for information gathering! Many of the books you will need for planning your research, such as dictionaries, thesaurus, encyclopaedia and atlases are all in the Reference Section of your library.

Finding specialised information can be confusing. If your research question is "Why did the dinosaurs die out?" you are unlikely to find that this is the title of a book! So you need to think about titles that could be helpful. Use the Dewey system for the non-fiction books, but be aware that many of these books are placed in categories according to how individual librarians believe they best fit. Using catalogue systems is the quickest way to the right information (unless you have a very kind and helpful librarian and even then they will use the catalogue to search!).

Most catalogue systems will allow you to search by author of the book, title of the book or by using keywords.

Have a look at Jamie's search results for *Mountains*:

Author	Title	Description
Black, M **Call No. 551.1**	'***Mountains*** Around the World'	Summaries of the 7 tallest ***mountains*** in the world. 55 pages.
Smith, B **Call No. 550.7**	'On Top of the World'	Descriptions of the most famous ***mountains*** for climbing. Includes tracks and statistics.
Gate, G. **Call Name: Gate**	'***Mountains*** of Ice Cream'	Jimmy likes ice cream so much he makes a ***mountain*** of it.

Jamie has searched using the keyword *mountains*. Every time it appears in the title or description that book has been added to his search results.

1. Are all the books on this list going to be helpful for Jamie's research? If not, which book will not help Jamie?

____

2. Why do two of the books have call numbers that come from the Dewey system and one has a call name?

____

3. Try doing a search for *mountains* on your library catalogue. Write the author, title and call number for the two books you think would be most helpful.

____

4. What problems can you see with Jamie's keyword?

____

Activity 24: Library Catalogues

Searching a library catalogue by keyword sometimes turns up books that seem to have nothing to do with your topic. There are lots of ways to make your catalogue search select books that are more specific. Jamie, who is looking for information about mountains, specifically wants information about mountains that people climb.

Have a look at some of the things he tries on the search page to help the catalogue sort out what information he wants. First Jamie tried:

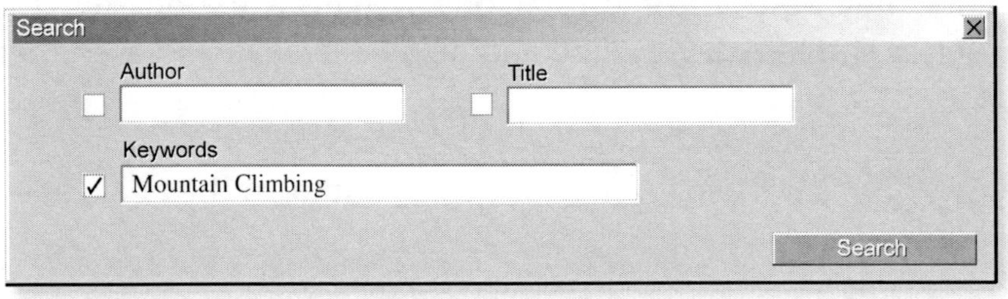

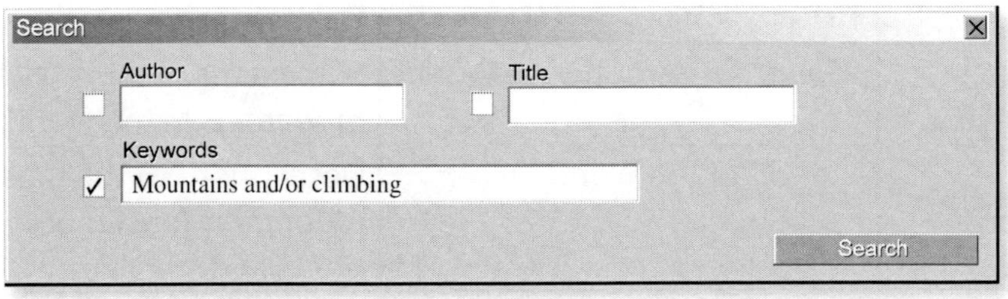

1. Which search do you think is going to be most successful? Why?
2. Try these searches yourself. See if your opinion changes.
3. Write down two of the books that turn up for you in these searches.
    - ______________________________
    - ______________________________
4. Did you come up with the same books as your friends?

Librarians are usually experts on how to search out information. When you have a search record showing what you have already searched under it makes the librarian's job much easier and quicker, so make sure that you keep one!

Try doing a keyword search on a topic of your choice with a friend. Keep a record of all the searches you do. Remember that spelling and punctuation does make a difference so make sure that your record shows your search term correctly! For example, try searching mountains with these words… *mountain* rather than *mountains*, and *mount*.

Activity 25: Internet Searching

Searching using the Internet can be tricky for a number of reasons:

- anyone can write anything on the Internet so that what you find may not be correct or even true
- some people have put really inappropriate things on the Internet
- some of the inappropriate things on the Internet come up under very normal and innocent keywords.

If you find that you have (by mistake) gone in to an inappropriate Internet site, turn the computer screen off immediately and find an adult to sort it out for you or follow your school guidelines.

The Internet is not classified in the same way as a library, so is always best to start your inquiry from a search page or search engine like Google. Your school might already have a preferred search page, so check with your teacher.

Toni is looking for information about rivers. Have a look at what came up on her search page when she searched for *rivers*.

Search for: rivers Search

Results Found *349,873* results:

1. All about **Rivers** in America
   … all you will ever need to know about great American **rivers** … **rivers** for cruising and canoeing…
   www.riverusa.com

2. **Rivers** for Rifles!
   …**Rivers** are the rifle people! Find out about a rifle store near you at…
   www.riversrifles.com

3. The Geology of **River** Formation
   …How **rivers** are formed… **rivers** have a unique formation caused by the…
   www.geoworld.com

Use this search page to help you answer these questions:

1. If Toni was looking for information about how rivers are formed, what site would have the most helpful information? ______________________

2. How can we tell that the second site would NOT be a good one for Toni to go to?

____

3. How many sites related to rivers were found? ______________________

4. Since Toni is looking specifically for information about how rivers are formed, what other keywords or search terms could she use? Write five alternatives search terms.

a__________ b__________ c__________

d__________ e__________

5. Try using these search terms. Do you get better results for Toni? __________

Activity 26: People, Email and Phone

Talking with people can be very valuable when researching. People, particularly experts in the topic you are researching, can:

- explain their actual experiences of your topic. (This is called a primary source because they have actually done it, or seen it and experienced it!)
- offer information and advice about where to find more information.

The amount of information and help you get from people will depend partly on how YOU ask them. Most people, when asked nicely, are willing to help or to tell you someone else who could help. When contacting people outside your school it is usually a good idea to let your teacher know beforehand. Ask your teacher if there is a particular way that you should approach an outside person for information. Your school may have a policy.

When contacting people it is really important to remember that you are likely to be dealing with strangers. Most people are very willing to be helpful. However, to be on the safe side:

- Don't give your surname, your first name will do. If they ask for a full name, check with your teacher. If they want to send you information have them send it to the school directly, care of your teacher.
- Don't give them personal details like your home address, unless you have asked your parents.
- If someone is making you uncomfortable end the contact politely but quickly and tell your teacher.

Have a look at this email. Can you spot three things that Kate has done wrong?

> Hi,
> I am doing a research study about volcanoes. I want you to send me some stuff about what you saw when you went to that eruption. I need it by next week.
> My home address is: 134/56 Cheeky Street, Silliville, Rude. 7090.
> Kate.

Things Kate should not have done…

1. ______________________________

2. ______________________________

3. ______________________________

Here is Jane's email. Is it better? Can you improve it even more?

> Dear Dr Lava,
> My name is Jane and I am studying volcanoes. I am in Year 8. I have read about your experience in the eruption on White Island last year and would be really interested in knowing more about what happened.
> I would really appreciate any information you could give me or any photos that you could send.
> I know you are busy and hope that this request won't take up too much of your time.
> My address at school is: Jane c/o Mrs Ball, Wise Intermediate, Politeville.
> Thanks very much for your time.
> Jane

Activity 27: Face-to-face Interviewing

If your expert is willing to be interviewed there are a number of things to bear in mind:

Interview Tips:

1. Be polite and friendly (in writing and face-to-face) this will help them and you feel at ease.
2. Before you meet them, make sure you've worked out the key questions that you need answers to or would like to know more about.
3. Ask your questions with enough time between each so that they have time to think and answer. Some of the best information comes from what people say when they've paused, had a think and start talking again.
4. Practise your interview beforehand so that you have an idea about how your questions sound. A teacher or parent might take you through the questions, and give you some tips.
5. How will you record the interview? On a tape recorder (make sure it works!) or through taking notes?
6. Start off by telling the person what you are researching, why, how they can help and the type of information you want. This will help them think about what they might be able to tell you.
7. Let your interviewee talk. Remember that your job is to LISTEN to what they say so that the next question you can ask is actually relevant or meaningful.

Here is a transcript (everything said written down) of some of Todd's interview with Mr Collins. Tick next to anything that shows a good inverview skill.

Todd — Interview with Mr Collins — 30/3/07

The Depression

Good Morning Mr Collins. Thank you so much for coming to help me to find out about what life was like for children in the Depression of the 1930s.

Lovely to meet you son. It's a pleasure to be able to help.

Would you like to come and sit down?

Thanks. My old legs just don't take as much walking as they used to.

Did you used to do a lot of walking?

I used to love a good walk. Of course during the Depression there wasn't any choice about it. No petrol so you couldn't drive anywhere, no spare parts so if your bike broke you couldn't fix it, no horses… we had a horse you know, used to keep it in the paddock out the back of our house but after a couple of years of no money and no food… well I guess some poor people just didn't care what they ate.

That sounds horrible!

Oh, Yes. They were very hard times for some people.

…pause…

What do you remember most about that time?

Hmmm… Probably the wonderful treat it was when we had butter for the bread at breakfast. And the way Mother would sometimes let us have the day off school to go out to the bush and trap rabbits. They were great days! Roast rabbit and tea made over a fire for dinner. Made me feel as rich as the King to have a rabbit to roast!

Compare what *you* thought Todd did well with what your friends thought he did well.

About Presenting Information

When students are ready to present their information they need to consider:

- who their audience is
- how best to explain what they have found out
- what presentation resources are most appropriate
- which presentation skills they have and which they need to build.

Learning to select the best medium or presentation method is a real skill. Where possible, teachers may like to steer students towards methods of presentation that fit their learning preferences.

It may help your students to have an 'Ideas for Presentations' board in your room. Encourage students to add their own ideas. Here are a few you may like to start with.

Ideas for presenting information

- Newspaper front page.
- PowerPoint presentation.
- Documentary (making a video).
- Designing an internet site (on paper or in reality if they have the skills).
- Posters.
- A reference book for other students.
- A story book for younger students.
- Demonstration and talk.
- Comic strip.
- Information application i.e. organising fundraising for a charity involved with their topic.
- Making a working model i.e. Hillside with the two armies in actual positions.
- Designing a museum exhibition with artifacts.
- Being interviewed by the class about topic – documentary style.

Activity 28: Presenting Information

When you are ready to present your information you need to think about:

- who your audience is
- how best to explain what you have found out
- what presentation resources are most appropriate
- which presentation skills you have and which you need to learn.

Jimmy has been looking at Disease Prevention for his research topic. From the information he found on how disease is spread, he realised that hand washing is of vital importance. His teacher has told his class that they are expected to present their research to the junior school. How do you think Jimmy could best share his research findings with young students? Write or sketch what you think he could do.

I think the best way to present this information is to:

Share your idea with a friend. What do they think? Have they got any suggestions to make about the presentation of your research? They might comment on:

- how well this would suit your audience
- how you could explain the ideas better
- whether it is original and interesting.

About Evaluation

Below is a list of things you may wish to use when you are looking at potential evaluation criteria for inquiry and research based topic studies. You may want to make a selection from the criteria rather than using them all. You also need to consider sharing this criteria with students at the start of their work so that they know what you are looking for in advance.

- Has the school/curriculum/agreed class process been followed?
- Does the student understand the rationale for the research and inquiry process?
- Has the student defined the topic?
- Were the keywords and phrases used to launch the inquiry/research?
- Are the keywords/phrases evident in their questioning?
- Is the questioning purposeful?
- Has the student's knowledge increased?
- Was the research planned rather than ad hoc?
- Have they been careful in selecting and crediting information?
- Have good records of their research been collected?
- Has the student successfully transferred information?
- Are notes ordered and comprehensible?
- Has any information 'lost the context' in which it was written?
- Have they used a variety of sources of information?
- Is there evidence of researching 'deeper' than immediate sources?
- Have they matched their presentation of findings to the audience?
- Is the presentation of findings 'balanced' (not too many or too much of anything)?
- Have they evaluated their work and sought ways to make it better?

Self evaluation of research projects

Peer evaluation of research projects can be a powerful learning medium. However this needs to be taught. It is unlikely that students will be able to feed back to each other effectively without being shown how. A good idea is to have a class 'Best Practice in Evaluating' meeting, and a discussion about the types of comments that are most helpful.

Peer evaluation should be seen as part of the research process (rather than something done at the end) and, as such, may be done several times throughout the course of an inquiry or research plan.

Activity 29: Showing Learning

Knowledge maps completed *before* we start to research a topic can help us identify what we need to find out. Mind maps completed *after* we finish researching a topic can help us understand how much we have learnt. When we compare the two maps we can evaluate our learning!

Have a look at my before and after maps. Compare them, then answer the following questions.

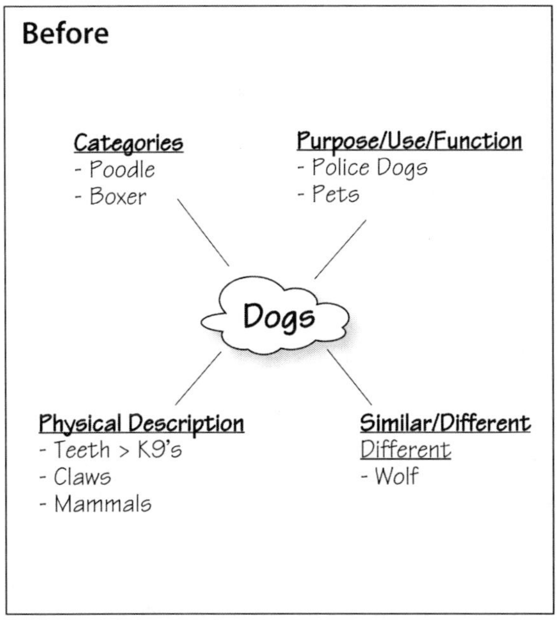

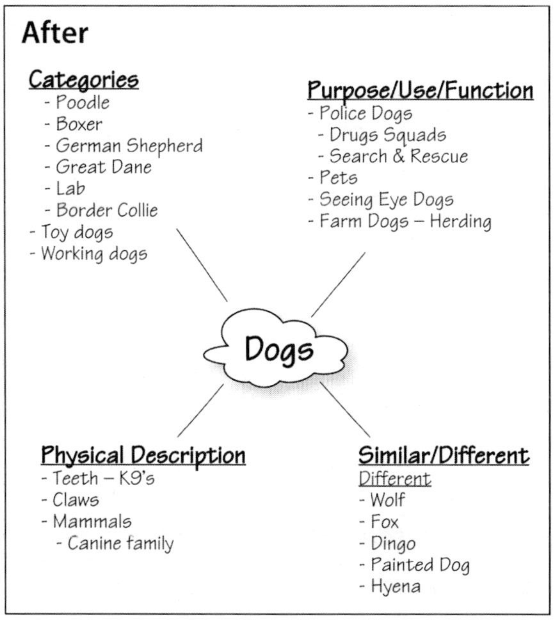

1. Have I have learnt much about dogs during my research?

2. What have I learnt the most about?

3. What have I learnt the least about?

4. What could I have found out more about?

5. How do you think these maps might help my teacher and parents?

Activity 30: Making Comments

When we evaluate something we are looking at it so that we can see:

- where things are up to
- what has been done well
- what needs more work
- what we may do next
- how well we have completed our purpose.

We can evaluate something when it is finished and also during a research or inquiry. For example, halfway through we may need to look back at what we have done, so that we can decide what to do next.

When we ask other people to evaluate our work by commenting on it they can tell us what they think has been done well or needs more work.

Similarly, when we are evaluating other people's work, it means we have been trusted to be fair and considerate in helping them to do THEIR best. Remember that everyone has different skills, so everyone's work should be different!

If you are asked to evaluate another person's work by commenting on it, it can be hard to know what to say. Look at these comments.

1. Put a line through the comments that you don't think would help someone know what they have done well or need to work on, and also through any comments you wouldn't like to see about your work.
2. Put a tick beside the comments that may help someone know what they could do to make their work even better.

"

Great note taking!

Only a dork would write that!

Your illustrations really help set the scene.

Your diagram is useless.

Wow! You must have spent hours in the library!

Have you thought of using colour pencil to add some colour?

Your Mum must have done this.

Your 'Diary of a Soldier' is so cool, it should be a book!

Have you thought about contacting NASA to see if they have more information about your topic? I found them really helpful.

Your PowerPoint was like a professional's… could you show me how to do that text effect?

Remember to check your spelling.

"

Discuss with your friends what comments you think would be appropriate and comments that you have liked.

Questions

Write the questions below again. You must ask for the same information but use a different question style to try and get better or more detailed information. (You don't need to answer the question, just ask it a different way!)

1. Why is the sky blue? ______
2. What do cats like to eat? ______
3. How do aeroplanes work? ______
4. When will the next Olympic Games be? ______
5. Are lions felines? ______

Extra for Experts

1. Is Mount Everest considered the most difficult mountain to climb? ______
2. What qualifications do you need to be a doctor? ______

Find the question starters listed below in the Word Find grid.

Why	**Are**	**Which**
When	**Will**	**Have**
How	**Can**	**Do**
Where	**What**	

H	I	F	C	D	P	V	D	V	K	J	F	A	V	W
S	Q	Y	M	C	N	Z	O	X	B	G	S	A	H	H
P	H	O	W	S	D	F	S	C	U	C	A	N	B	A
F	A	F	M	W	H	Y	D	F	G	M	Y	R	U	T
J	V	D	M	H	L	E	A	W	H	I	C	H	S	F
G	E	G	B	E	N	S	E	F	S	O	U	F	E	R
H	A	S	V	N	S	U	F	A	H	T	W	Y	D	J
K	I	D	U	T	D	F	A	W	A	P	I	O	G	C
L	S	K	K	O	G	T	R	O	E	J	L	E	U	R
N	A	S	W	H	E	R	E	V	S	F	L	S	H	B
X	N	F	A	V	U	X	Y	E	F	H	R	Y	R	I
M	O	T	D	S	H	O	U	L	D	L	H	G	L	H

Can you find two other question starters? What are they? ______ ______

Keywords Search Planning

Listed below are some topics that Jimmy needs to research. Help Jimmy with this first step in his research, list as many keywords under each as you can. (Use a dictionary and thesaurus if you wish to!)

Dogs	Beaches	Light
______________	______________	______________
______________	______________	______________
______________	______________	______________
______________	______________	______________

Keyword I.D.

Identify the keywords in each sentence. (You don't need to answer the question, just find out the subject!)

1. What do goldfish eat? ______________
2. What is the date of Christmas Day? ______________
3. Who invented scissors? ______________
4. When was the French Revolution? ______________
5. What are the rules of softball? ______________

Extra for Experts!

1. What is the rule in rugby about forward passes? ______________
2. Through what American states does the Mississippi River run? ______________
3. What should we do to plan for an earthquake? ______________

Sources of Information

Find the sources of information listed below in the Word Find grid.

E	N	C	Y	C	L	O	P	A	E	D	I	A	O	S
F	B	I	H	Y	K	V	D	A	E	P	O	P	S	E
B	G	N	O	T	E	L	E	P	H	O	N	E	N	N
O	L	T	V	B	M	T	I	M	G	S	B	O	Y	I
O	S	E	I	R	A	R	B	I	L	T	U	P	S	Z
K	O	R	D	K	I	J	N	F	X	V	I	L	N	A
S	N	N	E	P	L	R	E	P	J	H	K	E	D	G
G	M	E	O	H	I	N	T	R	A	N	E	T	Z	A
J	O	T	S	B	A	I	D	E	M	I	T	L	U	M

Encyclopaedia
Internet
Books
People
Magazines
Multimedia
Intranet
Email
Telephone
Videos

Can you find one other source that is not listed? ______________

Dewey System

Jane's reference books are in a mess so she wants to put them in order. Can you help her? The titles give you clues about the library section for each book. Check the Dewey system numbers below and number the books by topic. Example: 'Maths Maniac' would be numbered in the 500s for Maths and Science.

Maths Maniac	**Looking at Leonardo Da Vinci**
New Zealand: A History	**Speaking English**
The Geography of the World	**Hindu Religion**

The Dewey System

000	General
100	Philosophy and Psychology
200	Religion
300	Social Sciences
400	Languages
500	Maths and Science
600	Technology
700	Art
800	Literature
900	Geography and History

Notetaking

Take some notes about Rome. Use this title as your title, then use the keyword or phrase from each paragraph as your subtitle and finally make one or two points about what is written in each paragraph.

Rome

Legend has it that the city of Rome, in Italy, was founded around 753 BC by the twin sons of the god Mars, Romulus and Remus. Romulus and Remus were abandoned as babies, saved by a she-wolf and brought up by a shepherd. Remus was eventually murdered by his brother Romulus, who went on to rule Rome.

Rome was ruled by kings of Etruria until around 500BC when the Republic was formed. The Republic lasted until 27BC when Rome was again ruled by one man, an Emperor. The first emperor was Augustus.

Title: ____________________

Paragraph topic/Sub title: ____________________

____

____

Paragraph topic/Sub title: ____________________

____

____

Paragraph topic/Sub title: ____________________

____

____

Bibliographies

Tom did not keep a tidy list of the resources he used to do his research. Luckily he did write them all down! Can you help him to write out his bibliography? Remember to write books with author surname, then initial, the date it was published, the title of the book, the publisher and where it was published. Internet sites should be listed in Other Sources by their site address.

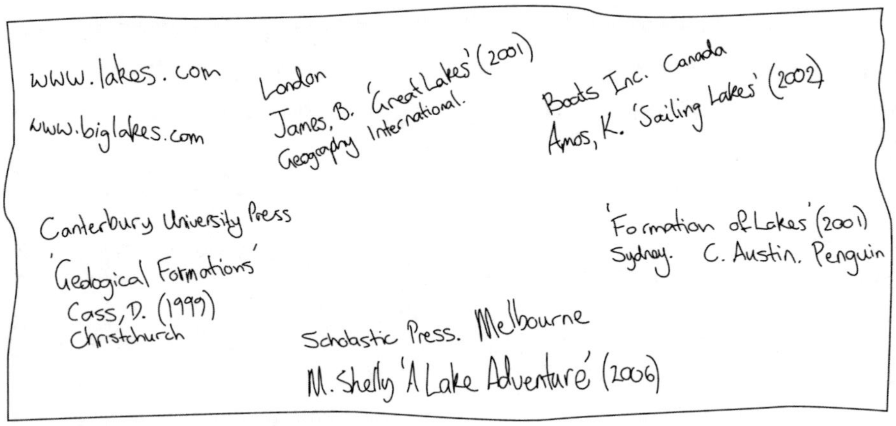
www.lakes.com
www.biglakes.com
London
James, B. 'Great Lakes' (2001)
Geography International.
Books Inc. Canada
Amos, K. 'Sailing Lakes' (2002)
Canterbury University Press
'Geological Formations'
Cass, D. (1999)
Christchurch
'Formation of Lakes' (2001)
Sydney. C. Austin. Penguin
Scholastic Press. Melbourne
M. Shelly 'A Lake Adventure' (2006)

Bibliography

____

____

____

____

____

____

Other Sources

____

____

____

Evaluation

Put a line through any of the statements that are NOT true. Evaluation:

- is only done at the end of a study
- helps you know what you are doing well
- has to be done 10 times in an enquiry
- can be done as often as you like but at least a couple of times during a study
- is a chance to tell people that you don't like them
- is a chance for your teacher to help you identify what skills you need to work on
- can help you to set goals for what to achieve next.

Write two comments that you think you would like to see on your work.

____

____

Finding People to Help

Look in your telephone book or a business directory for three organisations groups or people that could help you find information on:

Bricklaying

- ____________________
- ____________________
- ____________________

Animal protection

- ____________________
- ____________________
- ____________________

Scuba diving

- ____________________
- ____________________
- ____________________

Presentation

Although most presentation formats can be altered to suit your audience, some types of presentation are better suited to some audiences than others.

Have a look at the list of possible audiences, try to match the type or format of presentation with the audience that will be viewing or hearing the presentation. Draw a line between them.

Audience	Presentation Type
Large Assembly	Picture Book
School Hallway	Play
Junior School Children	PowerPoint
Parents and Family	Posters

Asking Questions

Our topic theme is...

The main question is...

Our subsidiary questions are...

Other questions that are important to understanding the main question.

Learning Areas and Specific Learning Objectives & Intentions

Learning Area: ______________________________

Specific Learning Objectives		Learning Intentions	Done/Assess
1. ____________	a)	____________	
____________	b)	____________	
____________	c)	____________	
____________	d)	____________	
2. ____________	a)	____________	
____________	b)	____________	
____________	c)	____________	
____________	d)	____________	

Learning Area: ______________________________

Specific Learning Objectives		Learning Intentions	Done/Assess
1. ____________	a)	____________	
____________	b)	____________	
____________	c)	____________	
____________	d)	____________	
2. ____________	a)	____________	
____________	b)	____________	
____________	c)	____________	
____________	d)	____________	

Learning Area: ______________________________

Specific Learning Objectives		Learning Intentions	Done/Assess
1. ____________	a)	____________	
____________	b)	____________	
____________	c)	____________	
____________	d)	____________	
2. ____________	a)	____________	
____________	b)	____________	
____________	c)	____________	
____________	d)	____________	

Skills Focus

Learning Experience Tracker

Learning Experience/Resource 1.

Name: ______________________________

Place to be done: ______________________________

Date to be done: ______________________________

Permissions/Notification attached: ______________________________

Links to Learning Intention: ______________________________

Purpose: ______________________________

____

Confirmation Sent: ______________________________

Resource returned/Acknowledgement sent: ______________________________

Learning Experience/Resource 2.

Name: ______________________________

Place to be done: ______________________________

Date to be done: ______________________________

Permissions/Notification attached: ______________________________

Links to Learning Intention: ______________________________

Purpose: ______________________________

____

Confirmation Sent: ______________________________

Resource returned/Acknowledgement sent: ______________________________

Learning Experience/Resource 3.

Name: ______________________________

Place to be done: ______________________________

Date to be done: ______________________________

Permissions/Notification attached: ______________________________

Links to Learning Intention: ______________________________

Purpose: ______________________________

____

Confirmation Sent: ______________________________

Resource returned/Acknowledgement sent: ______________________________

Assessment Task Tracker

Inquiry Topic: ______________________________ **Date:** ___/___/___

Assessment Name: ______________________________

Link to achieve objective: ______________________________

Assessed by: Teacher / Peer / Self
Method of Assessment: Written / Oral / Visual

Student Name	Date	Grade/Assessment	Notes

Student Inquiry: Prior Knowledge Map

Name: ______________________________ **Date:** ____/____/____

My topic is: ______________________________

Topic

____

When I look at this map of my knowledge, I can see that I could learn a lot about:

____

____

____

____

Student Inquiry: Post Inquiry Mind Map

Name: ______________________________ Date: ____/____/____

My topic is: ______________________________

Topic

____

When I look at this map of what I have learnt during my research I:

____

____

____

____

Student Inquiry: Notetaking Format

Name: ______________________________

Date: ______ / ______ / ______

Resource Name: ______________________________

____

Title: ______________________________

Sub Heading: ______________________________

- ______________________________
- ______________________________
- ______________________________
- ______________________________
- ______________________________

Sub Heading: ______________________________

- ______________________________
- ______________________________
- ______________________________
- ______________________________
- ______________________________

Sub Heading: ______________________________

- ______________________________
- ______________________________
- ______________________________
- ______________________________
- ______________________________

Sub Heading: ______________________________

- ______________________________
- ______________________________
- ______________________________
- ______________________________
- ______________________________

Sub Heading: ______________________________

- ______________________________
- ______________________________
- ______________________________
- ______________________________
- ______________________________

Diagrams/Images

Student Inquiry: Search Planning

Name: ______________________________ Date: ____/____/____

Topic:

____

Dictionary

Thesaurus

Encyclopaedia

Ideas for Finding Information

Books	Internet & Multimedia	People & Organisations

Student Inquiry: Search Recording

Search Term/Word	Title/Author/Site Address	Information Value

Things to note:

Student Inquiry: Presentation Plan

Name: ______________________ **Date:** ___/___/___

Topic: ______________________ **Due Date:** ___/___/___

Presentation Format (Circle one): Paper Poster PowerPoint Multimedia Video
Other: ______________________

Audience Format (Circle one): Students (Younger) Teacher Peers
Students (Older) Family Public
Other: ______________________

Presentation will include:

Non-Fiction: ______________________

Fiction: ______________________

Digital Resources: ______________________

Photos: ______________________

Diagrams: ______________________

Illustrations: ______________________

3D Models: ______________________

Demonstration: ______________________

Talk/Speech: ______________________

Other: ______________________

This presentation is intended to:

____

Student Inquiry: Evaluation

Name of Researcher: ______________________________

Evaluated By: Self Peer Teacher

Topic: ______________________________

Type of Presentation: Written Verbal Visual Multimedia
Other: ______________________________

Presentation shows evidence of research	Needs work	Good	Excellent
Presentation conveys information	Needs work	Good	Excellent
Care and thought have gone into the presentation	Needs work	Good	Excellent

The thing I like most about this presentation is: ______________________________

One thing I learnt from this presentation: ______________________________

Something to keep working on is: ______________________________

Comments: ______________________________

Signed: ______________________________
Date: ____/____/____

Information Evaluation

Use these questions to evaluate the information you gathered through your research.

1. What was the main question you were asking in your research?

2. What is the answer?

3. What did you learn that surprised you?

4. Where did you find your best information?

5. Which of your original questions are you still wondering about?

6. Which new questions do you have?

7. Where could you try looking for answers?

Reflecting on the Research Process

Consider the steps you followed when researching. To gain some perspective on your work, answer the following sentence stem below.

1. The easiest step was:

Because:

2. The most challenging step was:

Because:

3. The step that took the most time was:

Because:

4. I changed my plan in these ways:

5. Some things I would do next time:

6. I could have accomplished my goal by making more use of technology in these ways: